POPE LEO X

OPPONENT OF THE REFORMATION

SPECIAL LIVES IN HISTORY THAT BECOME

Signature LIVES

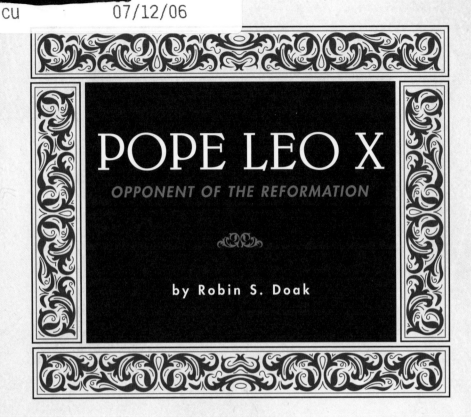

POPE LEO X

OPPONENT OF THE REFORMATION

by Robin S. Doak

Content Advisers: James F. Korthals,
Professor of Church History,
Wisconsin Lutheran Seminary

Dr. Michael J. Hollerich,
Associate Professor of Theology,
University of St. Thomas

Reading Adviser: Rosemary G. Palmer, Ph.D.,
Department of Literacy, College of Education,
Boise State University

COMPASS POINT BOOKS MINNEAPOLIS, MINNESOTA

Compass Point Books
3109 West 50th Street, #115
Minneapolis, MN 55410

Visit Compass Point Books on the Internet at *www.compasspointbooks.com*
or e-mail your request to *custserv@compasspointbooks.com*

Editor: Sue Vander Hook
Page Production: Bobbie Nuytten
Photo Researchers: Bobbie Nuytten and Svetlana Zhurkin
Cartographer: XNR Productions, Inc.
Library Consultant: Kathleen Baxter

Art Director: Jaime Martens
Creative Director: Keith Griffin
Editorial Director: Carol Jones
Managing Editor: Catherine Neitge

Library of Congress Cataloging-in-Publication Data
Doak, Robin S. (Robin Santos)
　Pope Leo X: Opponent of the Reformation / by Robin S. Doak
　　p. cm—(Signature lives)
　Includes bibliographical references and index.
　ISBN 0-7565-1594-7 (hardcover)
　1. Leo X, Pope, 1475-1521—Juvenile literature. 2. Popes—Biography—
Juvenile literature. I. Title. II. Series.
　BX1315.D63 2006
　282.092—dc22　　　　　　　　　　　　　2005025213

Signature Lives

REFORMATION ERA

The winds of change howled through Europe during the 1500s. The continent that had been united by the Catholic Church found itself in an uproar. In an attempt to reform the church, some people left the established religion, while others worked from within. The changes that began in Germany in 1517 when Martin Luther wrote his *Ninety-Five Theses* would transform everything. The Protestant Reformation's impact would be felt in all aspects of life—at home, in government, and in economics. Straddling the Middle Ages and the Renaissance, the Protestant Reformation would change the church, religion, and the world itself.

Pope Leo X

Table of Contents

SILENCE THAT PRIEST! 9

GROWING UP MEDICI 15

TEENAGE CARDINAL 23

LIFE IN EXILE 29

A MEDICI POPE 39

THE POPE AS POLITICIAN 47

A CHANCE FOR CHANGE 57

REIGN OF PLEASURE 65

PATRON OF THE ARTS 73

THE PROTESTANT REFORMATION 85

LIFE AND TIMES 96

LIFE AT A GLANCE 102

ADDITIONAL RESOURCES 103

GLOSSARY 105

SOURCE NOTES 106

SELECT BIBLIOGRAPHY 108

INDEX 109

IMAGE CREDITS 112

1 SILENCE THAT PRIEST!

Chapter

಄ೲഄ

Pope Leo X was annoyed with Martin Luther. The uproar about this German priest and the criticisms of the Catholic Church were a distraction. The pope was tired of what Luther was saying against the church. Leo had more important things to do, like planning an attack on Jerusalem.

But as head of the powerful Catholic Church, Leo could not completely ignore this priest. He appointed Catholic scholars to study Luther's criticisms—95 of them, to be exact.

In March 1518, Leo spent three days reading what priest Sylvestro Mazzolini Prierias had written about Luther. When he finished, he was convinced that Luther was guilty of heresy. There was no doubt he had seriously contradicted the teachings and the

In 1518, Italian artist Raphael painted this portrait titled Leo X and the Cardinals.

Frederick III, also called Frederick the Wise (1463–1525), was elector (ruler) of Saxony in what is now Germany. He protected Martin Luther, giving Luther's ideas a chance to spread throughout Europe. Frederick helped because he opposed the power of the pope and the emperor. He also didn't want Luther condemned to death as a heretic if his teachings were actually the truth.

laws of the Catholic Church.

In August, Leo ordered Luther to appear before him, but Luther refused. If the pope declared him a heretic, he might be permanently excommunicated from the Catholic Church or, worse, sentenced to death. Luther decided to stay in Saxony, where Prince Frederick III promised him safety.

Pope Leo was not pleased and demanded that Frederick turn Luther over to him. But Frederick refused. For two years, Leo generally ignored this priest who was largely responsible for the growing protest against the Catholic Church. On June 15, 1520, Leo could no longer disregard Luther. He had to attempt to silence him and put a stop to the rising opposition to the church.

Leo took his pen and officially condemned Luther and his radical opinions in writing. The papal bull, as the document was called, was the most official proclamation the pope could make. This one was called *Exsurge Domine (Arise, O Lord)*, titled after the first two Latin words of the official proclamation.

The bull began with these words:

> *Arise, O Lord, and judge your own cause.*
> *Remember your reproaches to those who*
> *are filled with foolishness all through the*
> *day.*

Leo identified those "filled with foolishness" as

Pope Leo X's papal bull, Exsurge Domine, *officially condemned Martin Luther and ordered his books and writings to be burned.*

Martin Luther and the followers who agreed with him. He called them "lying teachers" and accused them of heresy. Luther's ideas were a "deadly poison," claimed the pope. After listing 41 errors in Luther's writings, he declared:

> [B]ecause the preceding errors and many others are contained in the books or writings of Martin Luther, we likewise condemn, reprobate, and reject completely the books and all the writings and sermons of the said Martin.

Then the pope demanded that Luther recant, or take back, his accusations against the church. He went even further and ordered Luther's writings to be burned in public. Anyone who followed Luther would be thrown out of the church, the pope declared.

In December, Luther openly defied the pope. Outside the walls of the city of Wittenberg, Germany, he built a fire under a large oak tree. As onlookers watched, he burned Leo's *Exsurge Domine* along with the laws of the church and other papal documents.

The following month, on January 3, 1521, Pope Leo X issued yet another bull—the *Decet Romanum Pontificem*—officially excommunicating Luther from the church. Would that be enough to stop this outspoken priest and his followers?

Perhaps Leo had taken this priest too lightly.

Maybe he thought his ideas would eventually go away. How could one document, Luther's *Ninety-Five Theses*, have started such a huge spiritual revolution? Would things have been different if Leo had silenced Luther sooner?

Martin Luther openly defied the Catholic Church when he burned the pope's official document, the Exsurge Domine.

By ignoring Luther until it was too late, Leo left the Catholic Church on the brink of division. It was a split that would never be repaired. Leo X would be remembered as the pope who witnessed the start of what came to be called the Protestant Reformation, a movement that permanently divided the Roman Catholic Church. ‮‬

2 GROWING UP MEDICI

⸙∞⸙

*P*ope Leo X's parents raised him to be a spiritual leader in the Catholic Church. Even before he was born, they believed he was meant for religious life. The night before his birth, his mother dreamed her baby was a lion in a cathedral. She thought this meant her child would be a very important person in the church.

At Leo's birth on December 11, 1475, in Florence, Italy, he was named Giovanni de Medici. He was the second son in the richest and most powerful family in all Italy. When his ancestors arrived there in the late 1100s, they soon climbed to the highest ranks of society as merchants, bankers, and politicians.

Giovanni's father was Lorenzo de Medici, known as *il Magnifico* (the Magnificent). Although Lorenzo

As ruler of Florence, Italy, Lorenzo de Medici was surrounded by servants, adoring citizens, and exotic animals.

had no official rank or title, he ruled the entire city of Florence with his brother Giuliano. They inherited this powerful position from their father and Giovanni's grandfather, Piero, when he died in 1469. Lorenzo used his riches to help relatives, to set up young men in business and to support and encourage art and learning. Under his kind, generous leadership, the citizens of Florence experienced a golden age of prosperity, art, and culture.

Lorenzo de Medici wrote poetry, composed music, hunted, and indulged the citizens of Florence, whom he cared for deeply.

Giovanni's mother, Clarice Orsini, was a noblewoman from a Roman family. She married 20-year-old Lorenzo when she was 16. Over the years, they would have seven children: three sons and four daughters.

Giovanni and his siblings grew up surrounded by all the comforts that Medici money and power could buy. One of the family's homes was the *Palazzo Medici*—the Medici Palace. This gigantic home, built on one of Florence's most important streets, was taller than any other building in the area. It served as a reminder of Medici power to all who saw it. In back of the palace were beautiful gardens and the Medici menagerie, a collection of caged, wild, exotic animals.

Inside the palace, the walls were covered with artwork by some of the most respected artists of the day. Many of the paintings were portraits of famous historical and legendary figures, but their faces looked like members of the Medici family. Everyone living there added their own personal touches, choosing a piece of elegant furniture or a vase covered with semiprecious stones to furnish the lavish home. In the center courtyard was a famous statue made by the Italian sculptor Donatello. This large bronze likeness of David, the ancient king of Israel, showed him with a sword in his hand standing over the head of his enemy, Goliath.

Portrait of a young woman believed to be Clarice Orsini, the mother of Giovanni de Medici

The palace was also a place where important people throughout Europe came to visit and be entertained. Many feasts, banquets, and extravagant occasions were held there. Artists were invited to live at the palace and refine their skills. Lorenzo, the great patron of the arts, provided them with art supplies and a weekly salary, often supporting them for many years.

In 1490, when Giovanni was 15 years old, a young artist his age came to live at the palace. His name was Michelangelo Buonarroti. For two years, Michelangelo practiced his art in the beautiful Medici gardens. He drew pictures of the sculptures there and practiced sculpting. He carefully chipped away at a large, flat slab of fine white marble to create *Madonna of the Stairs*, a likeness of Mary and her infant son Jesus in relief on the flat surface.

Giovanni and Michelangelo became good friends. Neither one would have known then that Giovanni would one day become a valued patron of

Many talented artists surround Lorenzo de Medici, their patron and founder of a school for artists in Florence, Italy.

the artist. For the Medici family, sponsoring artists was more than just supporting the arts. It was also a way to become more powerful. The Medici would often send their artists to work for important rulers, which made these powerful leaders more likely to favor the Medici family. Whatever their motives were, however, the Medici family helped advance art and culture in Italy and throughout all Europe.

Michelangelo became one of the most famous artists of all time. He was a sculptor, painter, architect, and poet. Among his sculptures are the Pietà, David, Moses, and members of the Medici family. He is especially well-known for painting the ceiling of the Sistine Chapel and designing the dome of St. Peter's Basilica in Rome, Italy.

Education was also important to Lorenzo. He hired the best tutors in Italy to come to Florence and teach his sons—Giovanni, Piero, and Giuliano. Scientists, philosophers, musicians, and artists came to the palace and taught them there.

Their studies centered on Latin and Greek languages and literature. Giovanni was the family's most talented student. He was a quick learner and became especially interested in art and culture. Unlike his handsome brother Piero, Giovanni was a plain, stout child with a thick neck and round, bulging eyes. However, many commented on the beauty of his hands, which were "plump, white, and shapely." Later he drew attention to them by wearing beautiful rings with precious gemstones.

Giovanni de Medici grew up in the magnificent Medici Palace in Florence, Italy.

The intelligent and talented Giovanni received a lot of attention from his doting father. Lorenzo spent a great deal of time with his children. It was said:

> *[He] would forget the dignity of his office in romping with his children, for he would oftentimes indulge in any idle or childish amusement they might put him to.*

But like other wealthy fathers of the time, Lorenzo saw his seven children as ways to advance the Medici family fame and fortune.

Giovanni's sisters each married the husbands their father chose for them. The Medici were not royalty by birth, but Lorenzo did whatever he could to see that his daughters married noblemen.

Lorenzo had ambitious plans for his two oldest sons. Piero, the oldest, was heir to Lorenzo's fortunes. He would become the head of the family, the ruler of Florence, when Lorenzo died. For Giovanni, his second son, Lorenzo planned a career as a priest.

In 1482, when Giovanni was just 6 years old, he took part in a religious ceremony called a tonsure. As part of the ceremony, most of the young boy's head was shaved, except for a single band of hair around the circumference of his head. The ritual represented the family's commitment to dedicate their son to the church. It also was a symbol that Giovanni was not just a common person—he was now set apart for religious service.

The tonsure, from the Latin word meaning "to shave," showed that a man was dedicated and committed to the Catholic Church.

In 1483, 7-year-old Giovanni was made an abbot, the head of a monastery in France. Giovanni actually had no official responsibilities there. But now he was well on his way to a real leadership role in the Catholic Church. ❧

3 TEENAGE CARDINAL

❧❧❧

Only the best was good enough for the Medici family. If Giovanni was to be a leader in the church, then his father insisted that he be very important. As his son grew up, Lorenzo constantly talked to the pope about making his young son a high-ranking archbishop or even a cardinal, a position just one step below the head of the Catholic Church. He wanted Giovanni to be an adviser to the pope himself.

In 1484, when Giovanni was 8, a new pope, Innocent VIII, took over as leader of the Catholic Church. For the next several years, Lorenzo tried to persuade the pope to give his son an important position. When Giovanni was 10, he was named abbot of the monastery at Monte Cassino, a place about 80 miles (128 kilometers) south of Rome, Italy. Again,

The monastery at Monte Cassino has been destroyed four times, the last time in World War II when it was bombed by the Allies.

he didn't have any responsibilities, but he was paid for the position anyway. The title opened the door for appointments to more than 20 other religious offices he would one day hold within the church.

Lorenzo wanted even better for his son, but he needed a way to get close to Pope Innocent VIII. In 1488, Lorenzo found a way. His daughter Maddalena married the pope's son. Although priests and popes were not allowed to marry, many at that time had

Innocent VIII was pope of the Catholic Church from 1484 until his death in 1492.

children. Now Lorenzo had his connection. It would be easier for him to convince the pope that Giovanni should be raised up to a higher level in the church. Lorenzo kept after his new in-law, and he wrote letters and asked friends to convince the pope to promote his son. He called it his chief desire.

In 1489, Lorenzo got his wish. In March, 13-year-old Giovanni de Medici was appointed cardinal of the Catholic Church. The announcement was made in secret, however. Innocent VIII was worried that someone might object to the appointment of a young teenager to such an important position.

Giovanni de Medici was a cardinal in name only. He was not allowed to wear the clothes and symbols worn by other cardinals, and he had no real duties or authority. In fact, the pope made him leave Florence and attend the University of Pisa in Italy. He insisted that Giovanni study theology and canon law and learn everything he could about the religion and laws of the church.

Giovanni studied at Pisa for about three years, and in 1492, his position as cardinal was officially announced. At the age of 16, he walked out of a church in Fiesole, Italy, wearing for the first time all the red clothing and accessories of a cardinal.

Giovanni was now a member of the College of Cardinals, the official organization made up of all the cardinals of the Catholic Church. He joined the group whose most important jobs were to give advice to the pope and choose a new pope when one died. A successor pope was usually one of the cardinals. Although Giovanni was the college's youngest member, his fellow cardinals were quickly impressed with his maturity and serious nature.

The people of Florence were delighted that someone from their city was a cardinal. They celebrated Giovanni's important and powerful new role with a huge festival. There were feasts, shows, and parades to honor the son of their beloved ruler. Lorenzo was very ill with gout the day of the celebration. His joints hurt so badly that he couldn't get out of bed to attend the triumphal festival for his favorite son. Instead, he wrote him a special letter. He offered words of advice before Giovanni left Florence to go to Rome, the center of the Catholic Church. He warned his son about Rome, which he

The citizens of Florence planned a spectacular parade for Giovanni de Medici after he was appointed cardinal of the Catholic Church.

described as a hotbed of violent crime and treachery:

> *There will be many there who will try to corrupt you and incite you to vice [immoral conduct], and because your promotion ... at your early age arouses much envy. ... You must, therefore, oppose temptation all the more firmly. ... You are well aware how important is the example you ought to show to others as a cardinal, and that the world would be a better place if all cardinals were what they ought to be, because if they were so there would always be a good Pope and consequently a more peaceful world.*

Shortly after arriving in Rome that year, Giovanni received bad news. His 42-year-old father had died. He packed his bags and returned to Florence to bury the person he had counted on the most. ♆

Roman Catholic cardinals are distinguished by their bright red clothing, called vestments. The red color symbolizes their willingness to die for their faith. The vestments include a robe; a special mantle or cloak worn over the robe; a zucchetto, or small skullcap; a silk biretta, a square cap with three ridges; and a galero, a large broad-brimmed hat with at least 15 tassels. Cardinals with more positions and honors have more tassels. A cardinal also wears a special sapphire ring, which church members kiss as a way to greet and honor him.

EL TEMPIO

S. CROCE

S. MORRI

S. M. DE
LE GRAYE

S. GREGO
RIO

STE
PANO

CASTELLANI

POTE
RUBA

S. FELICITA

S. AP
STOLO

FONTE
UECHIO

PALAGIO
OLISPINI

PONTE A TRINITA

S. FELICITA

RRAIA

S. SPRITO

S. FRIANO

4 LIFE IN EXILE

Chapter

✎

After Lorenzo de Medici's death and while Giovanni was still in Florence, Piero took control of the city as planned. Giovanni's 22-year-old brother was handsome and athletic, but he was also an arrogant and hot-tempered ruler. He was not prepared to lead a city that valued its liberty and resented those who ruled with an iron fist. It wasn't long before he angered and alienated the people of Florence.

Piero was also having trouble with the government of France. When he signed a treaty with the French king to keep him from attacking Florence, the people were outraged at their leader. They thought it was a cowardly act. In November 1494, anger erupted into violence. The people were not just angry with Piero; they hated all three Medici sons. A raging mob

Piero de Medici (1471–1503) became ruler of Florence after his father died in 1492.

soon ran Giovanni, Piero, and Giuliano out of town.

Nineteen-year-old Giovanni fled for his life, disguised as a monk. Before he left, however, he managed to hide several valuable books from the Medici library under his robes. He also took time to pray. One person who saw the young man praying before he fled said, "I felt very sorry for him, for I reckoned him to be a worthy young man with excellent intentions."

The people took over the government of Florence and banished the Medici brothers from the city forever. Rewards were promised for anyone who captured Piero or Giovanni. For many years, the once-powerful Medici brothers wandered throughout Europe, waiting for the chance to return home.

In 1500, after living in exile for six years, Cardinal Giovanni de Medici went to Rome, where he thought he would be safe. In many ways, he picked up where his father left off. He lived a lavish lifestyle and decorated his home with fine antiques and art. He entertained and supported artists, musicians, and scholars. All agreed that Giovanni was the perfect patron and perfect cardinal—serious and educated, with a love of the arts and culture.

Giovanni soon discovered, however, that the way he was living took a lot of money—more than he had. Before long, he was borrowing money to keep up with his luxurious way of living.

Piero was not doing very well in his life of exile, either. He never saw his hometown of Florence again. In 1503, while serving in the French army, his boat overturned in the Mediterranean Sea just south of Italy, and he drowned. He became known as Piero the Unfortunate.

The death of Piero meant that Giovanni was now the head of the Medici family. Of course, he was a much different person than his hot-tempered older brother. He wanted peace and prosperity for his beloved city of Florence. However, he knew he would have to regain the trust of the Florentines in order to restore the power of the Medici.

Giovanni was willing to wait patiently in Rome until the time was right to rule Florence. In the meantime, he sent word to the people of Florence that he would not control their city by force. He even invited citizens to visit him at his magnificent home in Rome, and they came. All who visited found him a gracious and charming host who served the finest foods in elegant surroundings.

Giovanni also had to attend to matters in the Catholic Church. In 1503, the same year Piero died, the pope also died. It was now time for the College of Cardinals to do their most important job—elect a new pope. The cardinals selected Pius III, but he reigned less than four weeks before dying. They again had to choose a pope—this time, it was a man who would be called Julius II.

Julius' chief goal was to expand and strengthen the territories ruled by the church. These areas were called the Papal States. He often took land by force, which fittingly earned him the nickname "Soldier Pope." He enjoyed a military battle and often rode at the front of his troops.

To strengthen his influence, Julius formed what was called the Holy League, a group of military allies that included armies of the Holy Roman Empire, Spain, England, Venice, and Switzerland. Together,

Pope Julius II reigned as leader of the Catholic Church from 1503 to 1513.

they fought countries that were not part of the league. They drove the French completely out of Italy.

In 1511, Giovanni became actively involved in the battles. Julius appointed him representative to two Italian cities that were part of the Papal States. During a battle in April 1512, however, Giovanni was taken prisoner by the French. Fortunately for him, the Holy League defeated the French, and the young cardinal managed to escape, disguised as a soldier.

With the French defeated and with the help of Spain, the Holy League now turned its attention to restoring Medici power in Florence. Spain's ruler ordered the exiled Medici family to return as the city's new rulers. At first, the Florentines resisted. The city was enjoying a republican form of government that allowed citizens to have more control. But then Spain's army began marching toward the city.

Spanish troops entered Prato, a town north of Florence. There, Spanish soldiers looted and destroyed churches and other buildings, assaulting, torturing, and killing thousands of people.

The town of Prato, Italy, before the Spanish invasion of 1512

Giovanni wrote to Pope Julius:

> *This day, ... the town of Prato was sacked,
> not without some bloodshed such as could
> not be avoided. ... The capture of Prato, so
> speedily and cruelly achieved, although it
> has given me pain, will at least have the
> good effect of serving as an example and
> deterrent to the others.*

Once news of death and destruction in Prato reached Florence, the people quickly surrendered and changed their minds about the Medici. In September 1512, Giovanni rode triumphantly into the city of his birth after nearly 18 years of exile. Since he was a cardinal, the Catholic Church would not allow him to be Florence's new leader. But there was still his brother Giuliano. Before long, Florence accepted Giuliano as its ruler.

Giuliano de Medici (1479–1516) was the second Medici brother to rule Florence.

Giuliano, how-ever, was ruler of Florence in name only. He was more interested in entertaining and befriending the Florentines than ruling them. He loved wealth and luxury, gladly leaving the decision making to his older brother. Cardinal Giovanni de Medici held the real power. He would make decisions, and his brother would carry them out.

First, Giovanni did away with the city's republican constitution and restored the one his father had used. The people would no longer make decisions about how Florence was governed. He also established parliament, the lawmaking body. Members of parliament were ready and willing to please the Medici brothers. Nearly all the members were relatives or longtime supporters of the family.

Florence, Italy, home of the Medicis

It was important to support the Medici brothers. Giovanni didn't arrest or execute those who opposed

him. But he did take away their power by making sure they were removed from any official position.

One opponent to suffer this fate was Niccolo Machiavelli. For 12 years, Machiavelli had served Florence in a variety of political offices, and he had supported the people who drove out the Medici.

But when the Medici returned to power, Machiavelli was forced out of office. Then he was accused of plotting against the ruling family, thrown into prison, and tortured. Even under torture, Machiavelli swore that he was innocent.

Niccolo Machiavelli tried to improve conditions in Florence and encouraged a new style of politics.

Giovanni didn't have power in Florence for very long. Just five months after his glorious return to the city, he left once again. This time he wasn't forced out. He was on his way to Rome to again help select another pope. ✑

5 A MEDICI POPE

೧೪ళಿ

Pope Julius II died on February 21, 1513, after a 10-year reign. The College of Cardinals again convened to elect a pope. When the men met on March 4, they agreed on one thing—they didn't want another soldier pope like Julius.

It took seven days for the cardinals to come to a decision. On March 11, 1513, they agreed on a new pope of the Catholic Church—37-year-old Cardinal Giovanni de Medici.

Giovanni now had to choose the name he would use as pope. He could choose any name he wanted. Some popes chose the Latin form of their own name or the name of a previous pope or saint. A pope could also choose a name that described a certain quality, like innocent or pious. Giovanni chose the name that

The papal crown, formerly worn by Catholic popes, is often called the triple tiara because of its three-crown design.

nine other popes before him had used as far back as 440. He would be called Pope Leo X.

Unlike some earlier popes, Giovanni did not have to pay large sums of money to the cardinals to convince them to vote for him. They voted for the man they thought would make a worthy religious leader. One writer later described the new pope:

> He was esteemed chaste; his morals were excellent; and men trusted to find in him … a lover of literature and all the fine arts.

In other words, he seemed to be the exact opposite of the uneducated, aggressive Julius—just what the cardinals were looking for.

When news of the new pope reached Florence, the people were overjoyed. A Florentine pope would bring them great honor and power. They expected the Medici pope to look out for their interests.

For four days, the people of Florence celebrated. They lit bonfires, set off fireworks, rang bells, and

In 1271, cardinals of the Catholic Church couldn't decide who should be the next pope. They had been deadlocked for three years. Finally, Roman authorities locked them in a palace and gave them only bread and water until they could agree on a pope. It wasn't long before they elected Pope Gregory X, who then set up strict rules for future elections. Cardinals would be secluded without pay until a pope was elected. If they hadn't chosen someone after three days, they received only one meal a day. After five days, they got only bread and water. The rules were meant to speed up the election process.

fired cannons. Huge pageants and other festivities were enjoyed by all. In front of the magnificent Medici palace, large tables of food were set out for all citizens to enjoy. Wine was served from barrels covered with gold.

On March 19, 1513, Giovanni de Medici was officially crowned Pope Leo X. At the coronation, he was presented with the triple diadem, the crown worn by Pope Julius II and other popes before him. On April 11, the Catholic Church celebrated the new pope with bountiful, costly festivities.

The new pontiff, as the pope was called, was paraded magnificently through the streets of Rome. The city's fountains spouted wine instead of water as he passed by. Houses along the route were decorated with laurel, an evergreen with dark, shiny berries. The windows and doorways were draped with expensive

Painting of Pope Leo X's coronation by Giorgio Vasari (1511–1574) is located on a wall of the Vecchio Palace in Florence, Italy.

velvet cloth. Special archways were built throughout the city. The new pope passed through each one as he traveled throughout Rome. Each archway was more splendidly decorated than the one before it. Paintings and words of praise decorated the surfaces. Statues, antiques, and other treasures were placed in special nooks built into the arches.

The huge procession of soldiers, cardinals, and

Pope Leo X's coat of arms included the papal crown and elements of the Medici coat of arms.

important officials gloriously wound its way through the city of Rome. Each man was dressed in his finest clothing and robes. They made their way to the Lateran Palace, where many popes had lived.

The pope was last in the parade, where he rode in splendor on his favorite white horse. Eight men walked near the horse and rider, holding a canopy of embroidered silk to keep the pope from becoming too hot in the April sun. Still, the obese pope sweated profusely beneath his triple crown and jeweled cloak. Though uncomfortable in the heat, Leo reveled in the cheers and cries of the crowd as he passed by.

It was clear from the supporters who flocked to see Leo that many people had great hopes for this new pope. Most prayed that he would turn away from Julius' warlike ways and begin a period of peace. A representative of the emperor, who was the head of the Holy Roman Empire, wrote:

> *It is my opinion that the Pontiff will be gentle as a lamb rather than fierce as a lion. He will cultivate peace and not war. He will observe all his vows and engagements.*

But he added a word of caution:

> *Men change from hour to hour, and the Divine power often plays tricks with our human calculations.*

The people were ready for a new golden age in Europe. They looked forward to a time of luxury, learning, and peace. In a letter to Leo, the well-known Desiderius Erasmus, a scholar who criticized the Catholic Church, wrote his hopes for the new era:

[I hope it will be] a Golden Century, if ever anything can be golden, for in it I shall see ... the re-establishment of the

Desiderius Erasmus criticized the Catholic Church, but he hoped Pope Leo X would make changes that would improve the church.

*three principle assets of the human race:
a truly Christian piety, in so many ways
degraded; fine literature, hitherto either
neglected or corrupted, and an everlasting
concord of the Christian world, fountain
head and parent of piety and of culture.*

Erasmus' Golden Century did not take place. In coming years, it became clear that not everyone would support Leo. Later, one monk would suggest that the church paid a heavy price for electing this man. Those opposed to Leo would look back on the events that were about to happen and claim it was God's just punishment on the Catholic Church. ✆

6 THE POPE AS POLITICIAN

❧∞❧

As pope, Leo X established a disciplined daily routine. When he got up each morning, his secretary briefed him on the day's upcoming events. After several meetings with church officials, Leo attended Mass, the religious service of the church. Then he held audiences, or formal interviews with people who wanted to speak with him or win his favor. After this, Leo would have his largest meal of the day.

Following the meal, Leo rested briefly before holding more audiences. Later, he could relax and do whatever he liked. He often played chess and gambled with cards for hours. When the pope lost, he laughed cheerfully. When he won, he often tossed his winnings over his shoulders for onlookers to fight over. One person described him as enjoying "all with the delight of a spoiled child of the world."

Leo didn't forget his family and friends when he became pope. He wanted to make sure they benefited from his new position. He soon began handing out important offices to those close to him, regardless of whether they were suited for the job. He appointed his cousin Giulio de Medici to be the archbishop of Florence. This position put Giulio in charge of the Catholic Church in the area. He would later become a cardinal. Leo gave other positions to his younger brother and nephew.

The pope also hired hundreds of servants to take care of the large papal household. During his reign, there were nearly 700 servants, more than ever before. Many were friends, relatives, or members of Florentine families. The papal household was expensive. Leo spent twice as much money as the previous pope had.

Soon, Leo was forced to turn his attention to world affairs. The pope was not just a religious leader; he also had political power. One of his chief goals was to keep Florence—and Italy—independent. France and Spain were trying to gain control of parts of Italy, and Leo needed

As pope, Leo X gave generously to the less fortunate of Rome. He offered help and gave money freely to people who were sick, poor, or homeless. Hospitals and religious institutions such as convents and monasteries often received financial support from the pope. It has been said that he gave away more than 6,000 ducats, or gold coins, each year. One ducat was about 1/10 ounce (3.5 grams) of pure gold.

to do something about it.

In 1513, King Louis XII of France attacked Naples and Milan in Italy. To hold back the French king, Leo made a pact with the rulers of Spain, England, and the Holy Roman Empire. Together, the armies defeated Louis. The French king gave up all his claims to land in Italy and returned to France.

Two years later, however, there was a new king of France—Francis I. He also wanted to take control of Naples and Milan. To stop the young king, Leo again teamed up with his three allies. But Francis I proved tougher to beat than Louis XII. On September 14, 1515, the French king won the Battle of Marignano

King Francis I of France conquered the city of Milan, Italy, in 1515.

and took control of Milan.

Leo soon planned a visit to Bologna, Italy, where he would hold a conference with Francis. First, however, he planned to visit his hometown.

When word of the pope's upcoming visit reached Florence, many citizens sprang into action. Festivities were organized by two groups of noblemen: the Diamond Company led by the pope's brother Giuliano and the Branch Company led by Lorenzo, the son of the pope's late brother Piero.

*Francis I,
King of France
(1494–1547)*

In true Medici tradition, the festivities had to outshine any held before, and the two companies were ready for the challenge. More than 2,000 men were hired to work day and night to complete the preparations. Churches were used as temporary workshops, and houses were torn down to make room for decorations.

On November 30, 1515, Giovanni de Medici entered Florence for the first time as Pope Leo X. The Diamond Company held a huge triumphant procession modeled after ancient Roman parades held for generals returning home from victory. Three beautifully carved and painted chariots led the way. They carried figures representing Boyhood, Manhood, and Old Age. Each one also carried a motto: *Erimus* (we shall be), *Sumus* (we are), and *Fuimus* (we were).

Not to be outdone, the Branch Company doubled the amount of chariots to six. These chariots carried likenesses of famous Roman gods, politicians, and emperors. Oxen draped with decorative grass pulled

Leo X paraded magnificently through his hometown of Florence, Italy, as pope.

the first chariot. Twelve men dressed in furs rode nearby on horses beautifully adorned with gold cords and skins of lions, tigers, and wolves, whose paws had been dipped in pure gold. The other chariots were pulled by oxen, cows, and horses decorated with large wings. Water buffalo adorned with costumes that made them look like elephants also pulled the lavish chariots. Many distinguished people—priests, government officials, soldiers, poets, lawyers—proudly rode alongside on horseback.

The Branch Company had one more chariot in the procession—a spectacular one that carried a huge globe of the world and a young boy covered entirely in gold. He represented the Golden Age, a period of great splendor in Florence. Local artist Giorgio Vasari described the fantastic scene:

Italian artist Giorgio Vasari wrote about Pope Leo's visit to Florence.

In the midst of the float was a large sphere or ball, as it were the globe of the world, and on this was the prostrate figure of a man lying dead with his face to the earth, and wearing armour covered with rust. This armour was cleft [cracked], and from the figure there proceeded the figure of a child entirely naked, and gilded all over, to represent the age of gold reviving from the corpse of that of iron.

The young boy died, poisoned by the gold paint that covered his skin.

After the dazzling Florence celebration, Leo went on to Bologna, where he and King Francis I began working on a peace settlement. The pope was forced to do most of the giving. He agreed to hand over two cities in northern Italy and allowed the French king to submit names of people who should be appointed as church leaders.

Francis also demanded that Leo send him a valuable statue that had recently been discovered in Rome. Leo agreed but later sent him only a copy of the original.

In 1516, Leo and Francis finalized their agreement by signing a document called the Concordat of Bologna. On the way home from the meeting, Leo received bad news. Giuliano, his younger brother and ruler of Florence, was sick with

During Pope Leo X's reign, one of the most festive times of the year for the Catholic Church was the Carnival—a period of two weeks before Lent, the 40 days before Easter. Catholics attended parades, feasts, bullfights, dances, and parties. The pope and his cardinals often watched a contest between peasants in which they tried to catch pig-filled barrels as they rolled down a grassy hill. Some contests were high-class food fights, where people hurled oranges, eggs, flour, and water at each other.

tuberculosis, a disease that affected his lungs. He died on March 17, 1516.

Leo grieved his brother's death, but he quickly had to make sure a Medici was in charge of Florence. He did not hesitate to appoint his nephew Lorenzo as ruler of the city.

Leo also worked to keep control of land that belonged to the church. He had already lost some territory to the French king. Now Leo wanted to acquire even more land. He decided that the town

France fought many battles to take land from the Holy Roman Empire.

of Urbino in central Italy should become part of the Papal States.

In 1516, Leo went to war with Francesco Maria della Rovere, Duke of Urbino, and took the town from him. To ensure the townspeople remained loyal to him, Leo appointed his nephew Lorenzo ruler of the town. Lorenzo was now the new duke of Urbino as well as the ruler of Florence.

Leo was proving to be successful in world politics, but time would tell what he would accomplish for the Catholic Church. 🐦

A Chance for Change

7

When Leo became pope, he agreed to continue the Fifth Lateran Council, a meeting of cardinals, bishops, abbots, and other church leaders to discuss how to improve and strengthen the Catholic Church. The council met regularly during the first four years of Leo's reign. Many Catholics throughout Europe were eager for change and reform in the church, which they believed had become corrupt over the years. Many of its past and present leaders were guilty of corruption and wrongdoings, they said.

The council decided that the church needed many changes. But Leo wasn't interested, and he didn't carry out the suggested reforms. He allowed things to stay just as they were.

The council also ordered a crusade, a holy war

against the Muslim Turks. This was something Leo was very interested in. Planning a crusade was one of his favorite things. The empire of the Turks was made up of present-day Turkey, southeastern Europe, Syria, and Egypt. The Turks controlled Jerusalem, the city in present-day Israel highly honored by many Christians as a holy place where Jesus once taught and died.

For hundreds of years, the church had encouraged Christians to take part in crusades. They had fought many times for control of Jerusalem and the surrounding area called the Holy Land.

During his first year as pope, Leo raised money for his first crusade by selling indulgences. For a fee, a church member could buy an indulgence, an official document signed by the pope that was said to release a person from the penalty of sins and guarantee eternal life in heaven.

People could even buy indulgences for their dead relatives to shorten their time in purgatory. The Catholic Church taught that the dead waited in purgatory to get into heaven. Living family members

> The Crusades were expeditions made by Christians to the city of Jerusalem to deliver it from Muslim rule. During the 11th through 15th centuries, priests often announced a crusade in their sermons. After taking a solemn religious vow, each crusader received a cross from the pope and was then considered a soldier of the church. Crusaders were also granted indulgences, documents that promised forgiveness of sins, for fighting in these holy wars.

could pray for them or buy indulgences on their behalf so they could be released from the penalty of their sins and go on to heaven.

The price for an indulgence was based on how much money a person could pay. To Leo, selling indulgences seemed like the best thing for the church and the people—the church raised money for war, and people believed God had taken away the penalty of their sins and granted them eternal life.

At the last meeting of the Fifth Lateran Council, another crusade was approved, and Leo chose eight

Catholics purchased indulgences with the promise that they would be released from the penalty of their sins..

cardinals to plan it. They encouraged Leo to sell indulgences so they would have enough money for the war. The pope declared:

> There are many, and there will be many, who will gladly purchase eternal life for a small price, if they see that others are fighting for God in earnest, rather than pretending to do so.

However, some people started to doubt whether the crusade would ever take place. Money raised for some crusades in the past had been used for other things, and the crusades never happened. People also questioned the sale of indulgences. When Leo sent a notice about indulgences to France, the French representative responded:

> People have been deceived so often by [the offer of indulgences], from which nothing has resulted, that they now regard them as a deception, clever tricks to extract their money.

Large sums of money were raised, but a crusade never took place. The money was quickly spent on other things. Leo soon became the target of criticism. He had made some serious mistakes as pope, and his enemies were increasing. The Catholic Church was having financial problems. The previous pope had filled the church's treasury with large amounts of money, but Leo was quickly depleting it to support his lavish lifestyle.

Leo also had other troubles. Someone was trying to kill him. In 1517, several cardinals led by 22-year-old Alfonso Petrucci plotted his murder. At first, they planned to have him stabbed while he was out hunting. Then they decided that poison was a better way to kill him.

At the time of the plot, the pope had been advised

Alfonso Petrucci (believed to be the cardinal on the far left) was one of several cardinals who planned to kill Pope Leo.

to have surgery for a persistent medical problem. With the help of Leo's doctor, the men decided that they would apply poison bandages to Leo's skin after the operation. The poison would soak in through the skin and kill him. The Petrucci Conspiracy, as it came to be called, failed. The doctor was unable to convince Leo to have the surgery.

The plan was discovered, though, and the conspirators were caught and executed. Some cardinals who had merely known of the plot but said nothing were forced to pay huge sums of money to the pope to avoid punishment.

Leo now took steps to make sure he had plenty of support in the College of Cardinals. On July 1, 1517, he increased its size by appointing 31 additional cardinals. The change became known as the Great Promotion. Twenty-seven of the new cardinals were Italian, and all 31 were men Leo could count on to follow his wishes and orders.

Some of the men gave large sums of money to become one of Pope Leo's new cardinals. Although Leo benefited by packing the college with his followers and receiving extra money, it still weakened the church treasury. Now there were many more cardinals to support.

Other things were also draining the papal finances. Many people from Florence still depended on Leo as a patron, their financial sponsor.

An ambassador from Venice, Italy, wrote:

Leo appointed 31 cardinals in 1517 to make sure he had plenty of support.

> *The treasury of the Pope is empty because he is so generous that he does not know how to keep back any money; and the Florentines do not leave him a soldo [old Italian coin of little value].*

The pope was generous to many people, but it was hurting the Catholic Church. ᔓ

Euangelium Luce am xvi Cap.

8 REIGN OF PLEASURE

❦

After his first difficult years as pope, Leo finally tried to relax a little and enjoy himself. He loved to eat and host parties, and he used every possible occasion to hold a feast or festivity of some kind.

He often served unusual—and expensive—foods, including peacock tongue. For a surprise dessert, he would sometimes serve pies filled with live nightingales that flew out when the pie was cut open. Some much larger pies had little children inside who popped out when the pie was cut.

The pope often celebrated with a huge party on the feast day of Cosmas and Damian, the twin Catholic saints of medicine and science. One guest at the September 27, 1520, festivities described the merry affair:

A 16th-century artist depicts what he considered the luxurious and immoral lifestyle of Catholic clergy at the time of Pope Leo X.

> *[A]fter dinner he presented singing and
> playing, and the music was done in this
> manner: some fifty singers and players
> of various instruments, dressed as physi-
> cians, that is, with a long gown, partly
> pink and partly violet, and red stoles,
> came out two by two, led by Maestro
> Andrea and another buffoon, dressed
> up like ... the pope's physicians. They
> imitated them, cracking many jokes, and
> made everyone laugh.*

An easygoing, jovial man, Leo loved comedy, clowns, jokes, and a good laugh. He made sure a court buffoon, or clown, was around him at all times. Leo's favorite was Fra Mariano Fetti, who once told Leo, "Let's live, Holy Daddy, for all else is a joke."

Fetti once staged a fake joust for the pope's amusement. At the sound of trumpets, two knights ran through pots and pans that Mariano had placed in their paths. The cookware made such a clatter that people passing by fled in fear.

Leo enjoyed the entertainment of a good buffoon, but he also liked to be the jokester. Some of his jokes were quite cruel. They often made other people a laughingstock just for the sake of fun and amuse-ment. Once a monk performed a comedy the pope did not find funny. The unfortunate man was whipped and wrapped in a blanket while the pope laughed at the spectacle. Another victim of Leo's humor was the overweight poet Camillo Querno. When Querno became drunk with wine, Leo had him decorated with vines, cabbage leaves, and laurel. Then he crowned him "archpoet" and laughed at him until he cried.

Despite this display of unkindness, Leo was still

Pope Leo X was born in Florence, Italy, but moved to Rome, Italy, center of the Catholic Church, after he became pope.

Map shows present-day boundaries.

The Vatican

Rome

Papal Gardens

Sistine Chapel (completed in 1483)

wall

Basilica of St. Peter (completed in 1626)

St. Peter's Square (completed in 1667)

wall

AUSTRIA

SWITZERLAND

FRANCE

University of Pisa

Medici Palace

Pisa

Florence

CROATIA

BOSNIA & HERZEGOVINA

SERB. & MONT.

Corsica (FRANCE)

ITALY

Adriatic Sea

The Vatican (see inset)

Rome

Sardinia (ITALY)

Tyrrhenian Sea

N
W E
S

Ionian Sea

Mediterranean Sea

Sicily (ITALY)

0   100 miles
0   100 kilometers

considered very patient and kind. He was also known as a very religious man. Not all popes were extremely devoted to their faith. Some popes had bought their way into the position with their wealth and influence. Leo's father had used his power and money to get Leo where he was in the church, but Leo was still a serious man of religion. He believed that being the pope was a sacred responsibility that should not be taken lightly.

Most of the time, however, leisure activities were the most important things to Leo. His favorite activity was hunting, and he often spent up to six weeks in the fall at his country house just 5 miles (8 km) from Rome. At his Villa Magliana, as it was called, Leo could take off the red leather shoes traditionally worn by a pope and walk around in hunting boots. One of his men complained that wearing boots was

One of Pope Leo's favorite activities was hunting, or the chase, as it was called.

not proper, "seeing that then the people cannot kiss the Pope's feet!"

But Leo was there to enjoy the hunt. High on a hill, he would watch through a spyglass, waiting for an animal to fall into his trap or be captured in his net. When an animal fell into the trap, Leo would approach the animal and kill it with a spear. Many people knew about the pope's fondness for hunting. A Venetian ambassador wrote that "[Leo's] religious duties he fulfils conscientiously, but he likes to enjoy life, and takes an inordinate pleasure in the chase [hunt]." After a good outing, Leo was a happy fellow, willing to sign almost anything. His cardinals often took advantage of this.

Leo was also interested in nature, especially exotic species of plants and animals. Like his father, he built botanical gardens and had his own menagerie, one of the best in Europe at the time. His collection included lions, leopards, monkeys, parrots, and other creatures shipped to Rome from faraway lands.

One of his favorite animals was Annone, an elephant he received as a gift from King Manuel I of Portugal in 1514. Whenever the huge animal was brought before Leo, it kneeled down and saluted him by trumpeting three times. Then, to the pope's delight, the elephant filled its trunk with water from a nearby trough and sprayed the crowd.

Leo adored Annone, and he allowed the animal to

In addition to his gift of an elephant, the king of Portugal also gave Pope Leo X a rhinoceros. The gifts were intended to show his loyalty to the Catholic Church and gain the favor of the pope. As the rhinoceros was being transported to Rome in January 1516, however, the ship was lost at sea and believed to be shipwrecked. Leo never received his second gift from the king.

be led through the streets of Rome covered with jewels. Unfortunately, just three years after the elephant arrived in Rome, it died. In memory of the animal, Leo ordered the Italian artist Raphael to paint a life-size portrait of the elephant.

Although he enjoyed his leisure and entertainment, the pope also valued education and learning. He used money from the papal treasury to purchase books for the church library. His representatives traveled throughout Europe asking library owners if they could buy or copy rare manuscripts. Any owner who dared to refuse was threatened with excommunication from the church. Some books were copied and decorated just for Leo. One that contained Catholic chants and Latin songs was adorned with gold and rubies.

In 1515, Leo made the Roman Academy, a group of scholarly thinkers, into a university. He encouraged many top European scholars to teach there. But in spite of his love for intellectual debate and learning, Leo would not tolerate any debate about the Catholic Church. Throughout his reign, he ordered church censors to carefully examine any book that was about

Leo X served as pope (a word that means papa or father) from 1513 to 1521.

LEO . X . PAPA , FLORENTINVS,

to be published, as was common among governments at that time. Printers who produced books without the pope's permission risked having their printing presses and books burned in public. They also could be excommunicated from the Catholic Church. ❧

9 Patron of the Arts

>∞∾

On the day Leo was elected pope, he said, "Now that God has given us the papacy, let us enjoy it." One of the ways he intended to enjoy his reign was by supporting arts and learning. In 1515, he wrote:

> We have devoted ourselves to the govern-
> ment and extension of the Church, and,
> among other objects, we have conceived it
> to be our duty to foster especially litera-
> ture and the fine arts ... next to knowledge
> and true worship of the Creator, nothing
> is better or more useful to mankind than
> such studies.

Leo wanted Rome to be the cultural center of Europe. When people visited the city, he wanted them to see spectacular things that reminded them of the pope's glory and power. He supported architects, artists, poets, musicians, and others who flocked to Rome to make it a magnificent city.

The pope wanted to finish St. Peter's Basilica, the church next to the pope's residence where the church was based in Rome. Pope Julius II had started the project nine years earlier, and now Leo could imagine how beautiful it would be once it was finished. It would be an impressive sight for everyone who visited the city.

Italian artist Raphael (1483–1520) received financial support from Pope Leo X.

Leo strongly supported two of the greatest artists of all time—Raphael and Michelangelo. Leo's favorite was Raphael, whom he hired to decorate rooms in the basilica. On the walls and ceilings, Raphael created beautiful frescoes. He had a special talent for painting with watercolors on wet plaster. His paintings depicted Roman and Greek legends as well as Bible stories and historical events.

Raphael often substituted Leo's face for the faces of historical and legendary characters. In one fresco showing Attila, king of the Huns, being driven from Rome by Pope Leo I in 452, Raphael painted Leo X's face in place of the first Leo.

Sometimes Raphael's drawings were grotesque. Images of humans and animals were ugly, distorted, and strange. But most of his figures were cheerful, friendly-looking creatures.

Leo also made Raphael the supervisor of all ancient buildings in the city. The artist worked to preserve ancient statues and ruins throughout Rome. Many important sites and works of art were damaged, littered with garbage, or hidden by overgrown plants. Stones were being removed from the once glorious Coliseum to be used for the construction of new buildings. Raphael had a lot of ideas about how to restore the city, but many of them would not be accomplished in his lifetime.

The Coliseum in Rome was begun in 72 A.D. and dedicated in 80 A.D. It was 160 feet (49 meters) high, with 80 entrances. As many as 50,000 people at a time crowded into the Coliseum to be entertained. A popular event was the gladiator fights, where slaves, prisoners, and volunteers fought to their deaths. Other entertainment included wild animal hunts, mock naval battles, and lions killing Christians. After 404, most of these events were no longer held. But in the name of sport, lions, elephants, snakes, and panthers continued to be slaughtered there until the sixth century.

Michelangelo and Leo had known each other as teenagers when the artist lived at the Medici palace in Florence. Michelangelo had already become famous

Michelangelo (c. 1512–1579) once lived and worked on his art at Pope Leo's boyhood home in Florence, Italy.

for the paintings he had started for Julius II on the ceiling of the Sistine Chapel in Rome.

But Michelangelo was moody, sullen, and difficult to work with. A friend once told the artist, "You frighten everybody, even Popes!" Although Leo had fond memories of their boyhood friendship, he didn't get along with the artist now. So he gave Michelangelo a job as an architect in Florence, not as an artist in Rome.

Michelangelo's task was to design a façade, or front, for the church of San Lorenzo. He also designed and built a new sacristy inside the church, where holy vessels, clothes, and other religious items were kept. In 1520, Michelangelo designed the Laurentian Library in Florence to house Leo's large collection of books.

During Leo's reign, Michelangelo returned to Rome to complete his work on the ceiling and walls of the Sistine Chapel. Leo also wanted to decorate the lower walls. He ordered 10 tapestries to

be made in Brussels, the center for fine tapestry and rug making.

The heavy pieces of fabric with religious pictures woven into them were called the *Acts of the Apostles*. When they arrived in Rome, they were hung on the chapel's lower walls below Michelangelo's masterpiece. Each tapestry was based on a design drawn by Raphael.

The tapestries cost about five times more than what Michelangelo had been paid to paint the entire ceiling of the Sistine Chapel. When the tapestries were unveiled for the first time in 1519, an observer wrote that all "were struck dumb by the sight of these

Michelangelo painted the ceiling and walls of the Sistine Chapel in Rome, Italy.

Tapestries made for St. Peter's Basilica are now displayed in the Vatican Museums in Rome, Italy.

hangings, for by universal consent there is nothing more beautiful in the world." Some of the surviving tapestries can still be seen today in the Vatican Museums in Rome.

Leo was also a patron of musicians and instrument makers. He hired singers and composers from France and Italy. At one time, the chapel at Rome had a record number of 31 hired singers. Leo even liked to compose his own music, which was considered skillful for an amateur.

Wanting the best of everything, the pope hired a German trombone maker, Hans Neuschel, to create silver trombones. The skilled instrument maker was paid well.

Leo also loved the theater. He often ordered plays to be written and staged in honor of special people. They were performed with elaborate sets and scenery that were most often designed and painted by Raphael.

Leo's efforts made stunning improvements to the city of Rome. But they cost a lot of money, and the church treasury continued to shrink. Leo became known as the most extravagant pope in history. One of his officials wrote:

> [T]he Pope could no more save a thousand ducats [European gold coins] than a stone could fly up into the sky.

Leo had almost emptied the papal treasury. Finding money to run the Catholic Church was now a problem. Many Catholics were angry that the church was nearly bankrupt.

Leo had so much more he wanted to do. St. Peter's Basilica wasn't finished, but there was no money left to complete it. If he sold indulgences, he reasoned, there would be more money to support his projects and the church.

In addition, he decided to create more church offices so people could pay large sums of money to be appointed. Some positions were honorary, or merely a title, and the person had no duties to perform. For even more money, people could buy positions that required them to work, sometimes as a writer or a secretary. During Leo's reign, he sold about 2,000 of these offices each year.

Leo even created a new office that people could buy—knighthood. For about 1,000 gold coins, a person could be granted the honorary title of "knight." If the knight paid more money, he could have the title "count palatine" and receive a coat of arms, a family emblem or symbol often displayed on a metal shield during battle. Anyone with money could become a knight, but most knights were wealthy bankers.

As quickly as Leo raised money, he spent it. He continued to support scholars and artists. He rebuilt streets and buildings and freely gave money away. When he held his audiences, he made sure a bag full of money was always at hand. Before people left his

The pope had the power to grant knighthood to citizens.

presence, he dug into the bag and generously gave them some money.

But time and again, Leo ran out of money. He never seemed to have enough. Eventually, he started selling his own jewelry and borrowing money from bankers. But he still needed more.

In 1517, he decided that St. Peter's Basilica definitely had to be finished. Somehow he would collect enough money. The solution was obvious— the church had to sell more indulgences than it ever had before.

Johann Tetzel (c. 1465–1519) was a German priest in the Catholic Church.

Priests were told to preach often about indulgences from the pulpit. The push to sell these documents was not limited to Rome or Italy. It spread to many churches throughout Europe. One of the church's best salesman was a showy German priest named Johann Tetzel. Holding the papal bull announcing the sale of indulgences high on a velvet cushion, Tetzel entered German towns with a grand display and fiery sermons. Priests,

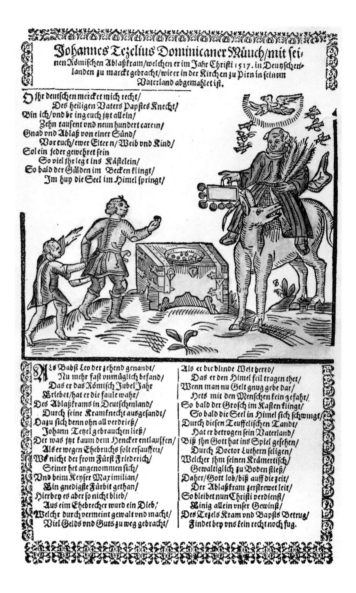

teachers, men, women, and children often met him with singing and a procession of flags and candles when he entered their city. Bells tolled and church organs resounded for this man with the documents that promised eternal life for the living and the dead. People could even purchase indulgences that paid for sins they had not yet committed.

People lined up to buy indulgences. But there were also many Catholics who were upset about the sale of what they considered to be cheap salvation and phony forgiveness. One German priest—Martin Luther—was especially concerned.

Luther had been bothered for some time by some of the church's actions. Now, he believed the sale of indulgences had gone too far, and he wanted to do something about it. By late 1517, he had heard enough about indulgences and wrote down his complaints against the Catholic Church.

That was just the beginning of what this man would do. For the next several years, he wrote against the church and the pope. He openly taught what he believed to be the true way to salvation—through faith in Jesus Christ, not through the church.

His ideas would challenge the pope and divide the Catholic Church forever. Many people would agree with what Luther said. His beliefs would affect all of Europe and eventually the whole world. ⌘

OPTIMO·PRIN
MED·IO
OB·RESTITVTA
VRBEM·AVGT

10 THE PROTESTANT REFORMATION

ⱥⱥⱥ

On October 31, 1517, Martin Luther nailed his *Ninety-Five Theses* to the door of Castle Church in Wittenberg, Germany. His document listed things he wanted to discuss about the Catholic Church, especially the sale of indulgences.

At this point, Luther had no intention of leaving the church or criticizing Pope Leo X. Before writing down his complaints, he said, "We now have a very good Pope, Leo X, whose integrity and learning are a delight to all upright persons."

But Luther wanted the Catholic Church to make changes. Posting questions and concerns on the church door was a common way to share opinions. Luther's theses invited university students and faculty to meet and debate the issues. But his

> More than 60 years before Luther posted his Ninety-Five Theses on the church door, Johannes Gutenberg finishing his printing press. From 1455 to 1500, more than 1,100 print shops sprang up throughout Europe, and more than 10 million books were printed. The printing press made it possible for people to read about new ideas and own Bibles and other books for the first time.

ideas soon reached a much larger audience. The invention of the printing press in the mid-1400s and the hundreds of print shops that had sprung up throughout Europe made it possible for Luther's ideas to spread to common people.

Someone must have copied the *Ninety-Five Theses* and delivered it to a printer. Thousands of copies soon spread all over Europe. People who questioned the church and resented it taking their hard-earned money to build grand cathedrals eagerly embraced Luther's message.

Leo didn't take Luther very seriously, though. He ignored him and took no action against him, hoping this outspoken priest would just disappear. But by doing this, Leo allowed the ideas to spread.

Luther continued to speak out against the church. Finally, Leo could no longer look the other way. In January 1518, the pope appointed three people in Rome to determine whether Luther had done any wrong. It didn't take them long to decide that Luther's writings were heresy.

The church ordered Luther's superior to make him

stop criticizing indulgences and to take back what he had written and said. He had four months to recant. Leo wasn't thinking much about Luther during those four months, however. He was planning a crusade he had long hoped to carry out. In 1518, King Francis I of France agreed to help the pope attack and reclaim Jerusalem. Leo was thrilled.

But other leaders of the church were still concerned about Luther's *Ninety-Five Theses.* That summer, Catholic priest Sylvestro Mazzolini Prierias published his opinion of Luther's work. After studying the document, he believed Luther was guilty of heresy on five points.

In 1517, German priest Martin Luther nailed his Ninety-Five Theses *to the door of Castle Church in Wittenberg, Germany, thus beginning the Protestant Reformation.*

When Leo read Prierias' opinion, he ordered Luther to appear before him. Luther wisely refused. The punishment for heretics was excommunication and usually death. Instead, Luther stayed in Saxony, where he was protected by Frederick III. When Leo demanded that Frederick turn Luther over, the prince flatly refused.

Frederick III of Saxony protected Martin Luther from possible arrest and execution.

Cardinal Cajetan, one of Leo's appointees, was also concerned about Luther. He was very worried about the deep rift that was forming between the Catholic Church and Luther's followers. In October, Cajetan left Rome to go to Germany, where he met privately with Luther. He ordered him to recant his heretical ideas and stop stirring up trouble. Luther would not do it.

In 1519, the split between Luther and the church became permanent. During a debate in Leipzig, Germany, Luther admitted that three of his 95 theses did not agree with the official teachings of the church. But during the same debate, he openly criticized the pope and the cardinals.

The Catholic Church was in crisis, but Leo still was ignoring the problem. Instead, he focused on European politics. Roman Emperor Maximilian I had just died in January, and Leo turned his attention to who would replace the ruler. The two favorites were Francis I of France and Charles I of Spain, but Leo didn't want either of them to become emperor.

Both men campaigned enthusiastically for the position and tried to gain the pope's support. Francis sent warships to threaten the Turks, hoping this display of military power would convince people that he was a true crusader and defender of Christianity.

But Leo wasn't interested in military might. He didn't want Francis or Charles to become more powerful than they already were. So he turned his support to Frederick III, the prince of Saxony and the man who had refused Leo's order to send Luther to Rome. Leo even tried to bribe Frederick with a gift to convince him to seek the position. The kings of France and Spain were furious. But when it became obvious that Charles I of Spain would be named Charles V, Holy Roman Emperor, Leo decided to clearly favor the Spanish king.

In the meantime, Luther was becoming even more outspoken. He published his *Address to the Christian Nobility of the German Nation* and other writings that encouraged German nobles to reform the church. He advised them not to honor Rome and

Spanish King Charles I was crowned Emperor of the Holy Roman Empire in 1519.

spoke out against many Catholic practices.

In November, Luther wrote an *Open Letter to Pope Leo* and sent him his pamphlet, *Freedom of a Christian.* The work, which was dedicated to Leo, was meant to reconcile the pope and the priest. It was "a token of peace and good hope," wrote Luther. He clearly explained his views on religion and asked the pope for "a spiritual and true freedom [that] ... makes our hearts free from all sins, laws and commands."

The letter to Leo also tried to assure the pope that Luther was still faithful to him. He wrote:

> *Therefore, most excellent Leo, I beg you to give me a hearing ... and believe me when*

*I say that I have never thought ill of you
personally, that I am the kind of a person who would wish you all good things
eternally, and that I have no quarrel with
any man concerning his morals but only
concerning the word of truth. In all other
matters I will yield to any man whatso-
ever; but I have neither the power
nor the will to deny the Word
of God.*

Luther's kind words, however, were followed by a stinging attack on the officials who surrounded Leo. He described them as depraved and godless. Leo was just a lamb surrounded by wolves, he said.

On June 15, 1520, Leo had had enough of this German priest. He officially condemned Luther's radical opinions in his papal bull, the *Exsurge Domine*. He declared:

*Portrait of
Martin Luther
(1515–1586)
by artist Lucas
Cranach the
Younger*

*A wild boar from the forest seeks to destroy
it [the Catholic Church] and every wild
beast feeds upon it. ... Moreover, because
the preceding errors and many others*

*are contained in the books or writings
of Martin Luther, we likewise condemn,
reprobate, and reject completely the books
and all the writings and sermons of the
said Martin. ... As far as Martin himself
is concerned, O good God, what have we
overlooked or not done? What fatherly
charity have we omitted that we might call
him back from such errors?*

The bull demanded that Luther stop writing, preaching, and disturbing the peace, unity, and truth of the church. Leo gave Luther 60 days to recant and obey the church.

In December, Luther received Pope Leo X's papal bull. In response, he burned it. Leo was outraged. How could anyone dare to burn his official declaration? On January 3, 1521, the pope wrote another bull, the *Decet Romanum Pontificem*. In it, he excommunicated Luther from the Catholic Church.

By February, it was obvious how most Germans were leaning. One person reported:

*All Germany is in an uproar. For nine-
tenths, "Luther" is the warcry; for the
rest, if they are indifferent to Luther, it is
at least "Death to the Roman curia [offi-
cials].*

The Catholic Church and the Holy Roman Empire continued to deal with this man who set the fires of

ICELAND

The Vatican
Rome — Papal Gardens — Sistine Chapel (completed in 1483)
wall
Basilica of St. Peter (completed in 1626) — St. Peter's Square (completed in 1667)
wall

Holy Roman Empire, 1500
Map shows present-day boundaries.

FINLAND

NORWAY
SWEDEN
ESTONIA RUSSIA
LATVIA
North Sea
DENMARK
Baltic Sea
LITH.
RUS.
BELARUS

IRELAND
UNITED KINGDOM
London
NETH.
Wittenberg
POLAND
BEL.
GERMANY
CZECH REP.
UKRAINE
LUX.
Worms
SLOVAKIA
Basel
AUSTRIA HUNGARY
ROMANIA
FRANCE
SWITZ.
SLOV.
CRO.
ITALY
BOS. & HERZ.
SERB.
& MONT.
BULGARIA
The Vatican (see inset)
Rome
Adriatic Sea
MAC.
ALB.
GREECE

ATLANTIC OCEAN

0   300 miles
0   300 kilometers

PORTUGAL
SPAIN

N
W   E
S

Mediterranean Sea

reform that soon spread throughout Europe. But Leo was still more interested in other things, like military ventures and hunting.

In late November, Leo suddenly came down with malaria while hunting at his country estate. On December 1, 1521, only a few days after becoming ill,

The Protestant Reformation started in Germany but soon spread throughout all Europe. Its effects were eventually felt all over the world.

he died. He was 46 years old.

Although Leo left behind a legacy of art and culture, he also left the Catholic Church in a mess. The papal treasury was nearly empty. By ignoring Martin Luther until it was too late, he left the church divided, a condition that would never be repaired.

Thousands of copies of Luther's Ninety-Five Theses were printed and distributed throughout Europe.

Perhaps Leo never understood the strength and seriousness of Luther's reform movement. Perhaps he didn't believe one person could possibly harm the powerful Catholic Church. Or maybe he was just more interested in other things.

History has not looked kindly upon this pope. Soon after Leo's death, Italian historian Sigismondo Tizio wrote his view of Pope Leo X:

> *In the general opinion it was injurious to the Church that her Head should delight in plays, music, the chase and nonsense, instead of paying serious attention to the needs of his flock and mourning over their misfortunes.*

Leo was buried behind the altar in the Church of Santa Maria sopra Minerva in Rome. His funeral was a small, simple affair. The little bit of money remaining in the papal treasury barely covered the meager funeral. Few people bothered to come to pay their last respects. Even scholars and artists Leo had supported over the years didn't show up.

Years later, Leo's nephew, Cardinal Ippolito de Medici, erected a large tomb for his uncle's body in the church. On the outside of the tomb was a plain sculpture of Pope Leo X. It wasn't extravagant like the Medici pope and patron of the arts it represented. But it did reflect the pope who experienced firsthand the darkest time for the Roman Catholic Church— the beginning of the Protestant Reformation. ঙ

POPE LEO X'S LIFE

1482
Takes part in a religious ceremony called a tonsure

1483
Made abbot of a monastery in France

1475
Born in Florence, Italy, December 11

1480

1474
Isabella becomes Queen of Aragon; known as the "First Lady of the Renaissance"

1483
Italian painter Raphael is born

WORLD EVENTS

1489

Appointed cardinal
in name only by
Pope Innocent VIII

1492

Becomes a member
of the College of
Cardinals

1490

1492

Ferdinand and Isabella
of Spain finance the
voyage of the Italian
Christopher Columbus
to the New World

1493

Maximilian I begins
reign as Holy Roman
Emperor

Life and Times

POPE LEO X'S LIFE

1500
Settles in Rome after living in exile for six years

1494
Banished, along with his two brothers, from Florence, Italy

1500

1497
Vasco da Gama becomes the first western European to find a sea route to India

1502
Montezuma II becomes ruler of Mexico's Aztec empire

WORLD EVENTS

1503

Helps select a new pope, Julius II

1512

Captured by the French army; escapes from captivity

1513

Selected pope; takes the name Leo X

1510

1503

Italian artist Leonardo da Vinci begins painting the *Mona Lisa*

1509

Henry, Prince of Wales, becomes King Henry VIII of England at age 18

1513

Vasco Nuñez de Balboa is the first European to reach the Pacific Ocean

POPE LEO X'S LIFE

1517

Orders the sale of
indulgences to build
St. Peter's Basilica
in Rome; Catholic
Church is criticized
by Martin Luther
in his *Ninety-Five
Theses*

1518

Plans a crusade to
reclaim Jerusalem

1515

Reorganizes the
Roman Academy
into a university

1515

1516

Erasmus pub-
lishes the New
Testament with
Greek and Latin
text

1517

The first Spanish
conquistadors, under
Francisco de Hernandez
Cordoba, reach the
Yucatan Peninsula

WORLD EVENTS

1520

Issues *Exsurge Domine*, the papal bull condemning Luther

1521

Issues a papal bull excommunicating Luther from the Catholic Church; dies December 1 in Rome, Italy

1520

1519

Ulrich Zwingli (1484–1531) preaches in Zurich and begins the Swiss Reformation

1524

German peasants rise up against their landlords in the Peasants' War, the greatest mass uprising in German history

DATE OF BIRTH: December 11, 1475

NAMES: Giovanni de Medici
Pope Leo X

BIRTHPLACE: Florence, Italy

FATHER: Lorenzo de Medici
(1449–1492)

MOTHER: Clarice Orsini (1453–1488)

SIBLINGS: Lucrezia (1470–1550)
Piero (1471–1503)
Maddalena (1473–1519)
Luissa (1477–1488)
Contessina (1478–1515)
Giuliano (1479–1516)

EDUCATION: University of Pisa
(1489–1492)

DATE OF DEATH: December 1, 1521

**PLACE OF
ENTOMBMENT:** Church of Santa Maria
sopra Minerva, Rome,
Italy

Additional Resources

Further Reading

Cole, Alison. *Eyewitness: Renaissance.* New York: Dorling Kindersley Publishing, 2000.

Saari, Peggy, and Aaron Saari. eds. *Renaissance & Reformation Almanac.* Detroit: UXL, 2002.

Shearer, Robert G. *Famous Men of the Renaissance & Reformation.* Lebanon, Tenn.: Greenleaf Press, 1996.

Wagner, Heather Lehr. *Medicis: A Ruling Dynasty.* Northborough, Mass.: Chelsea House Publishers, 2005.

Waldman, Nomi. *The Italian Renaissance: Daily Life.* San Diego: KidHaven Press, 2004.

Zelasco, Marco, and Pierangelo Zelasco. *Florence in the 1400s.* Chicago: Raintree, 2001.

Look for more Signature Lives
books about this era:

Catherine de Medici: *The Power Behind the French Throne*
ISBN 0-7565-1581-5

Desiderius Erasmus: *Writer and Christian Humanist*
ISBN 0-7565-1584-X

Martin Luther: *Father of the Reformation*
ISBN 0-7565-1593-9

William Tyndale: *Bible Translator and Martyr*
ISBN 0-7565-1599-8

On the Web

For more information on *Pope Leo X*,
use FactHound.

1. Go to *www.facthound.com*
2. Type in a search word related to this
   book or this book ID: 0756515947
3. Click on the *Fetch It* button.

FactHound will find Web sites related to
this book.

Historic Sites

Vatican City
Rome, Italy
Residence of Pope Leo X and other Roman
Catholic popes; site of St. Peter's Basilica,
the Sistine Chapel, and the Vatican
Museums

Medici Palace
Via Cavour, 1
Florence, Italy 50129
Birthplace of Pope Leo X, Giovani de
Medici

canon law
the rules of the Roman Catholic Church

crusade
a war fought for religious reasons, usually authorized by the pope

excommunicate
to remove as a member of the Roman Catholic Church

heresy
a belief that contradicts religious teachings

indulgences
documents signed by the pope and sold to church members that promised release from the penalty of sins

monastery
a building where monks live to carry out their religious vows

papal
relating to the pope of the Roman Catholic Church

Papal States
territories controlled by the Roman Catholic Church

patron
someone who gives money or support to someone, especially in the arts

theology
the study of religion

theses
ideas or statements made for debate and discussion

Source Notes

Chapter 1

Page 11, line 2: "*Exsurge Domine*: Condemning the Errors of Martin Luther." *EWTN.com*. 2005. EWTN Global Catholic Network. 06 October 2005. www.ewtn.com/library/PAPALDOC/L10EXDOM.htm

Page 12, line 6: Ibid.

Chapter 2

Page 19, line 26: Herbert M. Vaughan. *The Medici Popes*. Port Washington, N.Y.: Kennikat Press, 1971, p. 112.

Page 20, line 4: Ibid.

Chapter 3

Page 25, line 6: Christopher Hibbert. *The House of Medici*. New York: William Morrow & Company, 1975, p. 203.

Page 27, line 3: Ibid., p. 204.

Chapter 4

Page 30, line 7: *The Medici Popes*, p. 43.

Page 35, line 2: *The House of Medici*, p. 214.

Chapter 5

Page 40, line 10: *The Medici Popes*, p. 109.

Page 43, line 19: Ibid., p. 130.

Page 43, line 24: Ibid.

Page 44, line 6: André Chastel. *The Age of Humanism: Europe, 1480–1530*. New York: McGraw-Hill, 1964, p. 236.

Chapter 6

Page 47, line 15: *The Medici Popes*, p. 185.

Page 52, line 18: J.R. Hale. *Florence and the Medici*. London: Thames and Hudson, 1977, p. 84.

Chapter 7

Page 60, line 4: Norman Housley. *The Later Crusades, 1274–1580: From Lyons to Alcazar*. New York: Oxford University Press, 1992, p. 416.

Page 60, line 16: Ibid.

Page 63, line 2: *Florence and the Medici*, p. 85.

Chapter 8

Page 66, line 1: Bonnie Blackburn, and Leofranc Holford. *The Oxford Companion to the Year*. Oxford: Oxford University Press, 1999, p. 390.

Page 66, line 16: Paul Barolsky. *Infinite Jest: Wit and Humor in Italian Renaissance Art*. Columbia:University of Missouri Press, 1978, p. 96.

Page 69, line 1: *The Medici Popes*, p. 196.

Page 69, line 9: Ibid., p. 282.

Chapter 9

Page 73, line 1: Ferdinand Schevill. *The Medici*. New York: Harcourt, Brace and Company, 1949, p. 185.

Page 73, line 5: *Florence and the Medici*, p. 103.

Page 76, line 9: *The Medici Popes*, p. 219.

Page 77, line 13: Ibid., p. 236.

Page 79, line 13: Ibid., p. 182

Chapter 10

Page 85, line 8: Gregory Sobolewski. *Martin Luther, Roman Catholic Prophet*. Milwaukee: Marquette University Press, 2001, p. 59.

Page 90, line 6: John Dillenberger, ed. *Martin Luther: Selections from His Writings*. Garden City, N.Y.: Doubleday, 1961, p. 42.

Page 90, line 8: Brian P. Copenhaver and Charles B. Schmitt. *Renaissance Philosophy*. Oxford: Oxford University Press, 1992, p. 55.

Page 90, line 12: *Martin Luther: Selections from His Writings*, p. 45.

Page 91, line 26: "*Exsurge Domine*: Condemning the Errors of Martin Luther." 2005. *Papal Encyclicals Online*. 06 October 2005. www.papalencyclicals.net/Leo10/l10exdom.htm

Page 92, line 22: *Martin Luther, Roman Catholic Prophet*, p. 59.

Page 95, line 4: "Pope Leo X." 2005. *New Advent*. 06 October 2005. www.newadvent.org/cathen/09162a.htm

Barolsky, Paul. *Infinite Jest: Wit and Humor in Italian Renaissance Art*. Columbia: University of Missouri Press, 1978.

Bedini, Silvio A. *The Pope's Elephant*. New York: Penguin Group, 2000.

Blackburn, Bonnie, and Leofranc Holford. *The Oxford Companion to the Year*. Oxford: Oxford University Press, 1999.

Brion, Marcel. *The Medici: A Great Florentine Family*. New York: Crown Publishers, 1969.

Chastel, André. *The Age of Humanism: Europe, 1480–1530*. New York: McGraw-Hill, 1964.

Copenhaver, Brian P., and Charles B. Schmitt. *Renaissance Philosophy*. Oxford: Oxford University Press, 1992.

Dillenberger, John, ed. *Martin Luther: Selections from His Writings*. Garden City, N.Y.: Doubleday, 1961.

Fattorusso, G. *The Wonders of Italy*. Florence, Italy: The Barbera Press, 1930.

Gobineau, Arthur. *The Golden Flower*. Freeport, N.Y.: Books for Libraries Press, 1968.

Hale, J.R. *Florence and the Medici*. London: Thames and Hudson, 1977.

Hallman, Barbara McClung. *Italian Cardinals, Reform, and the Church as Property*. Berkeley: University of California Press, 1985.

Hibbert, Christopher. *The House of Medici*. New York: William Morrow & Company, 1975.

Housley, Norman. *The Later Crusades, 1274–1580: From Lyons to Alcazar*. New York: Oxford University Press, 1992.

Roscoe, William. *The Life and Pontificate of Leo the Tenth*. London: Henry G. Bohn, 1853.

Schevill, Ferdinand. *The Medici*. New York: Harcourt, Brace and Company, 1949.

Sobolewski, Gregory. *Martin Luther, Roman Catholic Prophet*. Milwaukee: Marquette University Press, 2001.

Vaughan, Herbert M. *The Medici Popes*. Port Washington, N.Y.: Kennikat Press, 1971.

Acts of the Apostles (tapestries), 77–78
*Address to the Christian Nobility
of the German Nation* (Martin
Luther), 89–90
Annone (elephant), 69–70
Attila, king of the Huns, 74–75

Battle of Marignano, 49–50
biretta (cardinal's square cap), 27
Bologna, Italy, 50, 53
Branch Company, 50, 51–52
Buonarroti, Michelangelo, 18–19, 74,
75–76, 77

Cajetan (cardinal), 88
Carnival, 53
Castle Church, 85
Catholic Church, 9, 10, 13, 21, 23,
32, 41, 45, 48, 53, 57, 61–62,
79, 85, 89
Charles I, king of Spain, 89
Charles V, emperor of Rome, 89
Church of Santa Maria sopra
Minerva, 95
Coliseum, 75
College of Cardinals, 25, 39, 40, 62
Concordat of Bologna (peace docu-
ment), 53
Cosmas (saint), 65
Crusades, 57–58, 59–60, 87

Damian (saint), 65
Decet Romanum Pontificem (papal
bull), 12, 92
Diamond Company, 50–51
Donatello, 17
ducats, 48

Erasmus, Desiderius, 44–45
excommunication, 10, 70, 71, 88, 92

Exsurge Domine (papal bull), 10–12,
91–92

Fetti, Fra Mariano, 66
Fiesole, Italy, 25
Fifth Lateran Council, 57–58, 59
Florence, Italy, 15, 16, 26, 29–31, 34,
35, 40–41, 48, 50–53, 75, 76
Francis I, king of France, 49–50, 53,
87, 89
Frederick III (prince), 10, 88, 89
Freedom of a Christian (Martin
Luther), 90

galero (cardinal's broad-brimmed
hat), 27
Golden Age, 52
Golden Century, 44–45
Great Promotion, 62
Greek language, 19
Gregory X (pope), 40
Gutenberg, Johannes, 86

heresy, 9, 10, 12, 86, 87
Holy Land, 58
Holy League, 32–33, 33–34

indulgences, 58, 59, 60, 81, 82–83,
85
Innocent VIII (pope), 23, 24, 25

Jerusalem, 9, 58, 87
Julius II (pope), 32, 40, 43, 74

knighthood, 80

Lateran Palace, 43
Latin language, 19, 39
Laurentian Library, 76
Leipzig, Germany, 88

Lent, 53
Leo I (pope), 75
Leo X. *See also* Medici, Giovanni de.
    appointments by, 48, 53, 54, 55,
        62, 79–80, 86
    art and, 40, 70, 73, 74–75, 76–
        78, 80, 95
    assassination attempt on, 61–62
    audiences with, 47
    birth name of, 15
    as composer, 78
    crowning of, 41
    Crusades and, 57–58, 59–60, 87
    daily routine of, 47–48
    death of, 93–94
    debt of Catholic Church and,
        48, 59, 60–61, 62–63, 70,
        79–80, 80–81, 94, 95
    election as pope, 39, 40
    expansion of Papal States by,
        54–55
    festivities and, 40–43, 50–53,
        65–66
    Fifth Lateran Council and, 57
    generosity of, 48, 63, 80–81
    health of, 93–94
    historical opinion of, 95
    as hunter, 68–69, 93
    Italian independence and, 48–49,
        50, 53
    literature and, 40, 70–71, 73, 76
    jewelry of, 81
    Martin Luther and, 9–10, 11–13,
        86, 87–88, 90–92, 94
    music and, 78–79
    name of, 15, 39–40
    nature and, 68–69
    papal bulls by, 10–12, 81, 91–92
    as patron, 62–63
    sense of humor of, 47–48, 66–67

    servants of, 48
    theater and, 79
Louis XII, king of France, 49
Luther, Martin, 9–10, 11–13, 83,
    85–86, 86–88, 89–93, 94

Machiavelli, Niccolo, 37
Madonna of the Stairs
    (Michelangelo), 18
Manuel I, king of Portugal, 69, 70
maps
    Italy, 67
    Protestant Reformation, 93
    Vatican, 67
Mass, 47
Maximilian I, emperor of Rome, 89
Medici, Giovanni de. *See also* Leo X.
    as abbot of Monte Cassino
        monastery, 21, 23
    art and, 18–19, 31
    birth of, 15
    as cardinal, 25–26, 31, 32, 35, 37
    childhood of, 16, 18, 21
    in College of Cardinals, 25–26,
        32
    debt of, 31
    education of, 19, 25
    exile of, 30–31, 32, 35
    festivities and, 26
    as head of Medici family, 31–32
    jewelry of, 19
    leadership of Florence and,
        31–32, 36–37
    as patron, 18–19, 31
    as prisoner of war, 33
    as representative to Papal States,
        33
    tonsure ceremony, 21
Medici, Giuliano de (brother), 19, 30,
    35–36, 50, 53–54

Medici, Giuliano de (uncle), 16
Medici, Giulio de (cousin), 48
Medici, Ippolito de (nephew), 95
Medici, Lorenzo de (father), 15–16,
    18, 19, 20, 21, 23, 24, 25,
    26–27, 68
Medici, Lorenzo de (nephew), 50,
    54, 55
Medici, Maddalena de (sister), 24
Medici menagerie, 17
Medici, Piero de (brother), 19, 21,
    29, 30, 31, 50
Medici, Piero de (grandfather), 16
Michelangelo (artist), 18–19, 74,
    75–76, 77
Milan, Italy, 49
Monte Cassino monastery, 23–24

Naples, Italy, 49
Neuschel, Hans, 78–79
Ninety-Five Theses (Martin Luther),
    9, 13, 85, 86, 87, 88

Open Letter to Pope Leo (Martin
    Luther), 90
Orsini, Clarice (mother), 15, 16

Palazzo Medici, 16–18
papal bulls, 10–12, 81, 91–92
Papal States, 32, 33
Petrucci, Alfonso, 61
Petrucci Conspiracy, 62
Pius III (pope), 32

Prato, Italy, 34–35
Prierias, Sylvestro Mazzolini, 9, 87
printing press, 86
Protestant Reformation, 13, 95
purgatory, 58–59

Querno, Camillo, 66–67

Raphael (artist), 70, 74–75, 77, 79
Roman Academy, 70
Rome, Italy, 19, 26, 31, 42–43,
    73–74, 75, 78
Rovere, Francesco Maria della, 55

San Lorenzo church, 76
Saxony, 10, 88
Sistine Chapel, 19, 76, 77
St. Peter's Basilica, 19, 74, 79, 81

Tetzel, Johann, 81–83
Tizio, Sigismondo, 95
tuberculosis, 53–54
Turkish Empire, 58, 89

University of Pisa, 25
Urbino, Italy, 54–55

Vasari, Giorgio, 52–53
Vatican Museums, 78
vestments, 27
Villa Magliana, 68

Wittenberg, Germany, 12, 85

About the Author

Robin S. Doak has been writing for children for more than 16 years. A former editor of Weekly Reader and U*S*Kids magazine, Doak has authored fun and educational materials for kids of all ages. She is a past winner of the Educational Press Association of America Distinguished Achievement Award. She lives with her husband and three children in central Connecticut.

Image Credits